LEAD

with

Distinction

A Guide for Planning & Realizing
a Meaningful Year as President

By Nancy Paulson

White Moments Design (DBA Rockport Web Sites)

PO Box 2446

Rockport, TX 78381

www.RockportWebSites.com

Efforts have been made to trace or contact all copyright holders. The publisher will be pleased to make good any omissions or rectify any mistakes brought to their attention at the earliest opportunity.

The word "Rotary" is a trademark of Rotary International.

Cover photography by Debbie High

Printed in the United States of America

Dedication

This book is dedicated to my husband, Dennis.

Always there, always believing, always pushing, always loving.

Table of Contents

FOREWORD

by Debbie High

I began my Rotary journey as a member of The Rotary Club of Amarillo, Texas in 2001. After a move to Corpus Christi, Texas in 2009 I transferred my membership to the Rotary Club of Southside Corpus Christi. "I missed the meeting," (some of you will know what I am talking about) and in less than a year I was asked to serve as President of the club. After attending Lone Star President Elect Training Seminar, I thought, "Oh my! What have I gotten myself into?" I realized just how much I still needed to learn about serving as a President of a Rotary Club, and I wondered how I would ever have the time to serve as an effective President. After serving as my club's President, my District 5930 leadership positions included, serving two years as an Assistant Governor, two years as the LT Governor Membership, and then District Governor 2016-2017. My Zone leadership positions include serving two years as an Assistant Rotary Coordinator Zone 21b and part of 27 and I have accepted an appointment from Rotary International President 2019-2020, Mark Maloney, as the Rotary Coordinator for Zone 25b and part of 29 Rotary Years 2019-2022.

It has been said the best "job" in Rotary is serving as President of your Rotary Club. I would have to agree. After all, as a Club President you will lead and motivate your club, ensuring club members feel appreciated, motivated, and a part of the Family of Rotary. It begins at the club level that we connect people, transform communities, and solve problems.

While attending PETS (President Elect Training Seminar) is the best required training for preparing you to serve as your Club's President, it is just the beginning of your education.

I first heard of Nancy Paulson when I moved to Rotary District 5930 and she was serving as our District's webmaster. It was not uncommon to hear one of my fellow Rotarians say, "Let's ask Nancy, she'll know." They were right. Nancy's formal training as an elementary school educator, technology coordinator, business owner of a thriving web and print design business, and her knowledge of the needs of Rotary Clubs and Districts enables her to successfully serve her fellow Rotarians.

I was very fortunate Nancy Paulson agreed to serve as my Governor's Aide when I was Governor Elect and Governor. In addition to the multiple formal required trainings I received, Nancy was instrumental in helping me get and remain organized for the year I served.

It was during this time we talked about tools that might be useful for Club

Presidents to better serve their clubs while making their "job" less stressful. The first was one of the first licensed Rotary District Apps, Rotary 5930, designed and developed by Nancy Paulson, and the second was the idea for this book, PE Leadership. I know the PE Leadership Book would have helped me immensely when I had the honor to serve as my Club's President. Congratulations! Now get busy planning as 1 July will be here before you know it.

Deborah G. High

American University Kogod School of Business, Business Executive Program
Rotary Coordinator, Rotary International Zone 25b & part of 29, 2019-2022
Secretary, Rotary Leadership Institute, Lone Star Division
Governor, Rotary International D5930, 2016-2017

PREFACE

by Nancy Paulson

The reason I wrote this book was based on my observations that many of the President-nominees and President-elect are overwhelmed by the scale and breadth of the job they are about to enter. They often are unable to use precious gift of time to plan, organize, & recruit others to assist. My background is variety, I was an elementary school teacher for 22 years, having earned: (1) Bachelors from University of Arizona, (2) Master of Arts in Educational Technology. With a career move for my husband, I had the opportunity to transition working into a Technology Coordinator (Systems Administration and training) for the teachers and staff at a large High School. In 2000 I retired from teaching and opened my own Web and Print Design business. The flexibility in my schedule allowed me to join Rotary. I have held club positions of Secretary, and Treasurer, a various Event chairs both at Club and District levels. I have been the Club Webmaster for my club since 2007. Additional I have been the District Webmaster for six of the last nine years. Three years ago, the incoming District Governor asked if I would be willing to serve as her Aide. During those years (her elect year and the year she served as Governor) my experience with the clubs of our District vastly increased.

Hopefully with this planning guide many clubs will be able to capitalize on the many opportunities while not being rushed or reinventing the wheel on issues we all face. I am about to serve my club as the President and needed to organize and prepare for "my" year. By putting it into a book form hopefully I can help you, your club, your community, and the District have greater success. Maintaining the weekly information and planning guide using the pages provided will hopefully allow you to focus your energies and do a more comprehensive timely and less stress inducing job.

So - find yourself a comfy location along with your favorite beverage and get started planning. Add more of your team members as you feel necessary.

Have a wonderful and exciting year as President!

Leadership

A good team of officers is important to the efficient running of your Rotary Club. The following provides brief descriptions of the role each officer should assume; however, all officers should be familiar with the duties of other positions as well as their own. Each officer should be familiar with club, district, and international constitutions, bylaws, and policies. The responsibilities in each club are different, so you should use this information as a guide to be elaborated upon.

President

The president of your club has two responsibilities which place this officer in a paradoxical situation. First, if a club is to be successful, the president must divide the responsibility of club leadership among fellow officers and club members. The use of delegated power is the only way to cope with large amounts of work in an efficient manner.

Secondly, the president must accept ultimate responsibility for club structure. In short, the buck stops here. So, at the same time the president divides the control of the club, responsibility must also be taken for the entire club operation.

Anyone who seeks the presidency should be mindful of this paradox along with several other considerations.

The president must understand that to be a leader means to work with people, not to be independent of them. Cooperation, understanding, and hard work are necessary to hold a group of young people together.

The president must also be aware of the foundations of Rotary. Being a Rotarian means operating upon a set of ethical principles; Rotarians follow "Service Above Self". These premises are the rules of the game, and if you are going to play the game, you must understand and abide by them. In addition, the president must set certain goals for the club and keep those goals in mind as the club progresses through the year.

The Effective Club President

1. Effective club presidents know where their time goes. They manage it rather than vice versa. Analyze your schedule and manage your time, so you will be productive and efficient by:

    a. Identifying and eliminating irrelevant things, things no one will really miss if they go undone.

    b. Deciding what you can delegate to someone else.

    c. Spelling out "time wasters" such as meaningless meetings and unnecessary communications and try to eliminate them.

2. Effective club presidents focus on outward contribution. In other words, they concentrate on results rather than the tasks themselves. Look up from your work and outward toward your goals. The club president lives and acts in two dimensions: (1) preparing for the future, and (2) building for the results long before they are achieved.

3. Effective club presidents build on strengths, their own and those of others. They acknowledge and accept their abilities and weaknesses. They are able to accept the best in others without being threatened. They help others grow by giving them opportunities and responsibilities. Feed opportunities and starve the problems.

4. Effective club presidents concentrate on the few major areas where superior performance will produce outstanding results. Set and stick to priorities. Here are some suggestions:

    a. Focus on the future as opposed to the past.

    b. Focus on opportunities rather than problems.

    c. Choose your own directions and listen to your own "drummer."

    d. Be an innovator and make a difference.

5. Effective club presidents make good, rational decisions. Here are some suggestions:

    a. Define the problem

    b. Analyze the problem

    c. Develop alternative solutions

    d. Decide the best solution

    e. Develop and implement a strategy that will convert the best solution into action.

Goals and Calendar

It is most important that the president, advisor, and the board of directors establish a plan of action for the year. The plan should include goals for membership, projects, tentative scheduling for meetings, projects and socials, as well as achieving recognitions. This planning must be completed to make committee assignments and for the treasurer to establish a budget. Once a plan of action is developed, then prepare a tentative calendar of club activities and deadlines. This initial plan of action is imperative to a club's success.

Delegating

Delegation is one of the most important aspects of a good president. You are only one person and cannot accomplish a successful year alone. It is always important to discuss delegation with your club advisor for guidance.

In the delegation process, remember these aspects:

1. Define clearly and creatively the responsibilities being delegated to each person, being sure to set limits while allowing flexibility.

2. Choose appropriate people for the assignment by placing people carefully, maximizing strengths and minimizing weaknesses. Seek out skills of your members.

3. Mutually set goals and time lines to be achieved. Expectations must be clearly defined.

4. Give accurate and honest feedback. People want to know how they are doing, and they deserve to know. This is both an opportunity for giving satisfaction and encouraging growth. Be sensitive when you deliver your praise or criticism; always be constructive.

5. Support your members by sharing knowledge, information and plans with them. It is incredible how many errors are made simply because of lack of information.

6. Whenever possible, give those who are responsible for completing assignments a voice in the decision making.

7. Really delegate! When given an assignment, most responsible people do not appreciate someone looking over their shoulder or taking back part of the assignment before they have had a chance to do it. Good leaders foster leadership in others by empowering them to be successful and allowing them to make mistakes. Make sure you guide while offering assistance and let go when appropriate and necessary.

When delegating specific duties and tasks, always emphasize the goals of your club and the assignment's overall impact on the success of your club. Be sure to establish times for progress reports. This will ensure that if the assignment is not being handled properly or the member needs assistance, the president and advisor can resolve the problem before it is too late.

Forums for Leadership

Leadership is exercised in many different ways. One of the most overlooked venues for leadership is in the context of meetings. As the presiding officer of your club, you can exert a great deal of positive leadership. Two types of meetings are the focus of your opportunity to exercise leadership: (1) the club meetings, and (2) the club board of directors' meetings. Both are important to effective leadership. You should take advantage of these forums to move your club toward the achievement of its goals.

Here are some suggestions about how you can use meetings to exert your leadership:

A. **Adjust your "style" to the group.** Horizontal leadership is preferred for your club meeting, whereas vertical leadership may be more appropriate for the board meeting. Horizontal leadership generally works better with a larger group. Treat each member as an equal. Use persuasive techniques. Preside in a positive, enthusiastic manner. Try to set the group at ease and make them feel like they are "center stage." Vertical leadership can be very boring and unproductive if the leader doesn't know what is going on or is distracted by efforts of certain members of the group to control the meeting. While a Rotary club is a volunteer organization, even volunteers can appreciate a leader who takes charge, particularly in decision-making situations. You should always build team spirit and keep the members focused on the goals of your club.

B. **Start with Board Meetings.** This is the most intimate leadership forum you will have during your year as president. Here are some helpful suggestions:

    a. Ensure the meeting place is comfortable for the group size.

    b. Choose a time when distractions and interruptions can be avoided.

    c. Have a well-constructed agenda with items for decision clearly outlined (this should be reviewed with the advisor for guidance well before the meeting).

    d. Make every attempt to complete business in the time allotted.

    e. Prepare before the meeting for any special reports or information which may be needed for the group's work.

    f. Express appreciation to the individual members, advisor, and the group as a whole for their contribution to the achievement of your club's goals.

C. **Exercise the courage of leadership.** Sometimes individual members of the group need to have their thoughts and actions redirected in order for the group to function properly. Have the courage to move discussion along even if it means confronting a member whose actions distract from the group. If you have an opinion that has not been expressed, carefully introduce your idea. Count on others in the group to see the merit of your suggestion. Allow the group to "brainstorm" solutions to problems without letting the meeting degenerate into wasted time and effort. A courageous leader molds the group into a vibrant decision-making body.

D. **Follow the agenda while allowing sufficient time and enthusiasm for "brainstorming."** At the beginning of the meeting, ask each person if there are any items to add to the agenda. Assure people that each item will be handled on a consensus basis. Make sure each person is involved in the process. Involve those who may seem "to be somewhere else." Call for decision as soon as you detect a group consensus. Don't belabor points or allow the group to stray off the subject.

E. **Be a good listener.** Leadership is related to "followship." You cannot be effective if your contact with the membership is weak. Most leaders fail because they enjoy speaking more than listening. Be able to paraphrase each member's comments and restate the group's consensus when it appears. By listening, you can identify and solve problems within the group and help them move toward completion of tasks.

F. **Be effective in presiding at club meetings.** Here is a major forum for making an impact on your club during your year as president. Each time your club meets, they look to you for the leadership that will make the meeting a meaningful part of the life of the club. Take this forum and your responsibilities as the presiding officer seriously. Have an agenda and adhere to it. Remember that the members have given the club a certain part of their life (time). Be positive and enthusiastic about what is going on. Listen to the responses of the members about the "state of things." Above all, be prepared to take the necessary steps to ensure a good productive meeting.

G. **Don't take yourself too seriously.** You are going to make some mistakes as the presiding officer. If you "goof," recognize it and admit that you're good, but getting better. Work to make sure the members feel good about your leadership, even when things don't go as smoothly as you would like.

H. Be prepared. Stay ahead of the game by communicating effectively with all your officers and members. Let them know what you expect from them and listen to what they expect from you. Anticipate future events and keep your members aware of upcoming activities. Use every appropriate means available to make what you do at meetings effective and productive.

Meetings can be significant forums for your leadership. Don't take them for granted. Use them to help your club achieve its goals during the year. When the year is over, you want your members to make the unavoidable conclusion, "Wow, our president did an excellent job. We've had a great year."

"If your actions inspire others to dream more, learn more, do more and become more, you are a leader."
-John Quincy Adams

"Innovation distinguishes between a leader and a follower."
-Steve Jobs, Apple co-founder

"Do not follow where the path may lead. Go instead where there is no path and leave a trail."
-Ralph Waldo Emerson

"Leaders instill in their people a hope for success and a belief in themselves. Positive leaders empower people to accomplish their goals."
-Unknown

"Leadership and learning are indispensable to each other."
-John F. Kennedy

Why Plan and Organize?

So why is planning and organizing hot? Why is everyone telling me to get it done? It's your way to demonstrate that you are thoughtful and can think ahead — that you are not just about the big idea, but also about its execution. This is a powerful dichotomy to possess as a leader — the ability to not only be a visionary, but also have the drive to achieve the vision.

Don't let what may feel like the tedious nature of sitting down to plan and organize stop you from achieving greatness as the leader of your club for a year. Let's consider what you can do today to get cozy and snuggle up to Planning and Organizing:

1. **Get clear on the strategic objectives and mission of your parent group** — You need to know why you are performing a task and how this links to the larger direction for where you are going. Otherwise, why do it at all? *(Read the insert about Strategic versus Operational Plans on the next page.)*

2. **Identify clear milestones/goals** — There needs to be clear markers along your project's way that ensure you are making progress in the direction of your end goal. For this I recommend starting from the end and working your way backwards.

3. **Identify and prioritize resources** — Based on the work required, determine the resources you need. Be realistic in terms of headcount, budget, and time. Have a backup plan in case your resources fall short. Are you going to move around the deadlines, reduce scope and deliverables, etc.?

4. **Get feedback** — While it's faster to work in a vacuum, you could be missing something. Share your plan with others and get another set of eyes to check for your missing details.

5. **Revisit the plan regularly** — Ensure you are tracking progress on a regular basis. Your plan may need to be adjusted or you may have to go to your back-up plan.

The more specific you are in planning, the better it may be for you. However, don't get so wrapped up in the planning that you lose sight of what you are trying to do, but be sure that any problems that might arise are identified and that solutions are pre-determined.

Keep in mind that the most important factor in the success of the planning process is the plan itself. At the end of the process, you need to ask questions to show that you have a good plan:

- Is the plan clear? Do we understand it?
- Does the plan agree with the values and purpose of the organization?

- Does it identify the items of importance to our club?
- To what extent does it contain specific, measurable goals and objectives?
- Is the plan a real basis for action?
- Does the plan contain contingencies in case of a serious internal or external event?
- Does the plan include a way of obtaining feedback on its success?
- Is the plan flexible in case it needs to be changed?

What makes a great leader? One thing is certain: Leadership doesn't depend on your title; it stems from how you act.

An effective leader doesn't have to be outgoing or have the loudest voice in the room. People with quiet, low-key personalities can also be outstanding leaders. True leadership is not about self-promotion. It is the ability to get others to follow what you are advocating: To trust you; to respect you; to feel that your vision and strategies are in everyone's best interests—not just your own.

Strategic vs. Operational Plans

Are they the same? If not, what's the difference? Do you need both? We hear these kinds of questions frequently. In short:

A **strategic plan** outlines your mission, vision, and high-level goals for the next three to five years. It also takes into account how you'll measure those goals, and the major projects you'll take on to meet them.

An **operational plan** (also known as a *work plan*) is an outline of what your club will focus on for the near future—usually the upcoming year.

Simply put, your strategic plan shares your vision for the future, while your operational plan lays out how you'll get there on a daily/weekly/monthly basis.

Membership Matters

There are two main reasons people join:

1. Friendship
2. Local impact.

If you add in

3. Development & Training, Personal/Professional recognition; Professional Networking.

95% joined for "local reasons"!

International is important – BUT people join for LOCAL reasons.

When we say "local reasons" we need to think like an individual, not a club. Local isn't just a neighborhood hands-on project. Local means getting to know influential people and community leaders, bonding with neighbors and colleagues, people close-by. Learning about local issues and becoming involved.

What do you think Rotarians said about why they stay in Rotary?

Same two reasons:

- Friendship is clearly the #1 reason why people stay in Rotary
- If you add in impact my community, networking, personal and professional recognition and training opportunities; all things local are still about 85% of the reasons people stay.
- Global Impact - International appeal comes naturally with Rotary experience and knowledge.

People are attracted to Rotary for:

- Friends and Contacts
- Local impact
- Engagement of one's skills and passion
- Working with and learning from leaders

To sustain growth, clubs/organizations need to know why business and professional people join and why they stay. If invitees don't join or members don't stay, our club is not meeting or exceeding their expectations.

If you club isn't attracting and retaining members effectively: **Reach out to District, Zone and/or International for assistance.**

Membership Matters

1. **Think Local.**
   - International will come

2. **Provide Friends and Contacts.**
   - It's the #1 reason people stay in Rotary.

3. **Know The Name and Vocation of each member.**
   - You can't have friendship with other members if you don't even know their names.
   - You can't have pride in the club and in members if you don't even know what they do.

4. **Develop Leaders.**
   - A Rotary Club is a leadership organization, not just a friendship or service club – that's what makes us special & different from other groups!

We are helping members become better leaders,
And in that process
We are helping communities become better communities.

Fifty Ways to Recruit New Members

Clubs are always looking for ways to grow and recruit new members, There are many things club members can do in order to attract new members. Here, you'll find a fifty viable approaches that one could use in order to recruit more members.

1. Ask someone
2. Bring a guest to meetings
3. Advertise in newspapers & cable TV
4. Have a clear club goal & a strategic plan
5. Letters or personal contact with local businesses
6. Contact with Chamber of Commerce
7. Place customized bookmarks in library books
8. Have public meetings at malls, outdoors, etc
9. Have a booth at malls, fairs, festivals etc.
10. Place pamphlets in doctors' offices, hospitals, cafeterias, libraries, etc.
11. Host an Open House
12. Hold a club assembly only on membership
13. If you have a Rotary Club, ask Rotary Foundation alumni to join
14. Give the membership chair one minute at every club meeting
15. Make the membership chair a club director
16. Put together guest information packets
17. Service projects that serve a need in the community
18. Invite family members to join
19. Send letters to people in the news with an invitation to visit the club
20. Print club business cards with club meeting location and time
21. Distribute extra copies of magazines that relate to your club in waiting rooms, etc (i.e.: Rotarian)
22. Hold high-profile meetings
23. Hold wine and cheese receptions for prospective members
24. Have a special guest day
25. Send club members to district membership seminar
26. Make prospective members feel important
27. Honor outstanding community members with awards
28. Don't take age into consideration
29. Make some meetings social events
30. Build a club web site
31. Use group email to promote your club
32. Put posters in public areas
33. Ask corporations and employers to sponsor or subsidize membership
34. Have a reward program for those who bring in new members

35. Create more fun
36. Give a money back guarantee—if after 3 months a new member does not want to be a club member, return their fees
37. Invite the media to cover well known speakers
38. Use word of mouth
39. Network with coworkers, friends, and family
40. Follow up with guests
41. Place a colored dot on the watch of every member to remind them to bring a guest
42. Lead by example—how many members have you recruited?
43. Have members give talks at other organizations
44. Provide guests with free meals
45. Update your club's classification survey
46. Look for members in ethnic groups not represented in your club
47. Provide brochures for new employee packets in members companies
48. Advertise at sports events
49. Ask the district for help
50. Hold joint meetings with other groups

Research shows the following – 90% of people who join a club do so because a friend invited them to do so. 90% of club members have never invited anyone to come to a meeting, let alone join. Build that bridge to fix that problem and recruitment problems are over.

Find more ideas by going to the book's website resources at www.RockportWebSites.com/LeadWithDistinction/

Membership: Looking beneath the surface.

Successful Strategies for Recruiting and Retaining Members

Club Membership Plan

Recruiting new members is one of the most important things you can do for the future of your club. Develop a formal recruitment plan, set recruitment goals, develop strategies and then follow through. Communicate the plan to members and provide regular progress reports.

Recruitment Process

Make sure your members know the membership selection criteria and the process for recruiting new members. Produce a flier for members which spells out these procedures clearly and simply. Keep the flier updated and accessible.

Each One Reach One

Make it a personal honor that each member proposes at least one new member to the club. All members are responsible for identifying and inviting prospective members; indeed the future of your club depends on it.

Bring A Friend Service Activity

Rather than inviting guests to a regular meeting consider inviting them to participate in a club service activity: a working bee, sausage sizzle or similar. This gives prospective members a different view of Rotary and enables them to see first hand its contribution to the community.

Prospective Members Kit

Develop a prospective members' kit, with information about your club, its members, successful service activities and the like. Make it easy to read and visually appealing. Make sure the kit includes a 'call to action', something the reader can do to find out more about Rotary membership.

Welcome New Business

Send a letter of congratulations and welcome to proprietors of new businesses in your area. Let them know about Rotary and give them a contact point if they would like to learn more about the organization

Find more ideas by going to this book's website resources at www.RockportWebSites.com/LeadWithDistinction/

Fun Ideas for Short Segments During Rotary Club Meetings

1. "WHAT YOU DIDN'T KNOW ABOUT ME" SEGMENT

(Jenny Coburn—Australia) Our club has a WYDKAM segment. It is very often humorous, and always pretty amazing! One member each meeting is given 2-3 minutes to reveal something about themselves that other members probably don't know.

2. QUESTION OF THE WEEK SEGMENT

(Eszter Horvath-Papp—England) At Bristol Bridge Rotary Club we used to have a "question of the week". We were a fairly young club (ages 20 to about 45) with a relatively high turnover of members, and with members occasionally bringing along friends and colleagues. Therefore, it was important for us to have something that would enable everyone to have a few moment to speak and to reveal something about themselves which wasn't simply their name and their employment. The question would only be revealed at the beginning of the meeting, and we would go round the room and everyone would give their answers. We found the answers were usually light-hearted and often prompted subsequent discussions, and enabled even the most shy person to become known to everybody. It was also really interesting to find out new things about people that we thought we knew well! Some of the questions included:

- what was your favorite children's program when you were little?
- if you could have a superpower, what would you like?
- tell us about a memorable holiday?
- what was your most embarrassing moment?
- if you were made president of the world what would you do first?

3. FLASH CARDS SEGMENT

(Trinda L. Ernst - Canada) One of our most enjoyable activities included a "flash card" segment. Each member is given a silly card (our cards feature a vulture on a beach) and when members encounter other members around the town, or in the meeting, they can flash their card and the other member has 30 seconds to produce their own card (from wallet, pocket, car, purse, etc.). If the card isn't produced quickly enough (in the set time e.g. 30 seconds), the flashed member has to pay a $1 fine at the next meeting. One person flashed his minister in church and another person caught someone while driving, so we had to introduce more rules to avoid traffic accidents! If it isn't fun, it isn't Rotary!

4. PRESENTATION ABOUT AN INTERNATIONAL ROTARY CLUB SEGMENT

(From Warrnambool Daybreak) In rotation, each member has to research and prepare a short presentation or talk on some other Rotary club in the world e.g. where they are, how many members they have, what projects they do etc. This info and photos can easily be found on the web. The same member has to think up and prepare a short fun activity for the club members to do during the meeting and this can be related to the featured club (e.g. at the recent DG visit, the featured club was located in the Caribbean, so the fun event was a short Limbo dance)

5. A TOAST TO AN INTERNATIONAL ROTARY CLUB SEGMENT

(From Maryborough Rotary, Victoria) Each member of the club is invited to prepare some information on another Rotary Club in the world and propose a toast to that club at the start of our meeting. The information typically includes: the name and location of the club, what District they are in, the number of members, where and when they meet, what are two of their current projects, and the name of their current President. To present the toast, our members usually wear a hat or item of clothing related to the place of the club.

6. POKER GAME SEGMENT

(From Alamogordo Rotary) We just started a "Poker Game" where it will last for six weeks at a time. Each week you come to the meeting, you will get one playing card (you get two if you bring a friend). At the end of six weeks the member with the best five card poker hand will win a prize.

7. HAPPY BOX INSTEAD OF FINES SEGMENT

(From Swan Hill Sunrise, Victoria, Australia) Instead of having fines, Swan Hill Sunrise has a "Happy Box" (e.g. a funny piggy bank) that is passed to each member who places a coin in the "box" and briefly announces something they are happy about on that day. The good thing about this is that it forces everyone to think of something positive and something for which they are grateful—a great way to start (or end) a day.

8. ICE BREAKER QUESTIONS SEGMENT

(From Jessica Wittman, Rotary Club in Muscatine, Iowa) Spend 5 minutes asking Icebreaker questions such as, What was your first car? What was your Prom (Deb Ball) theme and what did you wear? How did you propose/get proposed to? What were name choices for your children that did not get picked? etc.

9. BATTLE OF THE SEXES QUIZ SEGMENT

(From Jessica Wittman Rotary Club in Muscatine, Iowa) Spend 5 minutes with a Battle of the sexes trivia quiz. Pull 5 women and 5 men from the group. The men have to answer questions women would know (hair, makeup, fashion etc.) Women would have to answer questions men would know (sports, cars, home repair etc.)

10. 50/50 TICKET DRAW SEGMENT

Have two tickets drawn in a "raffle" and there are different "contests" or feats to accomplish before you win the "pot" e.g. the first to inflate a balloon, build a pyramid of cards, sink a putt, say a tongue twister or a myriad of other fun tasks.

11. CELEBRATE A CELEBRITY BIRTHDAY SEGMENT

Use the Internet to discover birthdays of famous people falling on the days of your Rotary club meeting. Ask something like "Famous birthdays for April 1st" etc. Have your Fun Director, the Sergeant or a member from a member roster to announce the birthday and do something related to the person e.g. play one of their songs, read one of their short poems, read an extract from their book or a speech or show a picture of what this person has done.

12. CELEBRATE A SPECIAL DAY SEGMENT

One of the easiest way of coming up with fun events for your club meetings is to relate them to the various International and National Days or Weeks. You can use one of these "days" as a theme for a whole meeting, or simply as a short fun activity during the meeting. You can find lists of International Days on www.daysoftheyear.com, (every day of the year has multiple options) and it's also in Facebook under "Days of the Year". You can also type "International Days" in a search engine Here are some typical days from February with some ideas for events or activities:

February 9th—15th: Random Acts of Kindness Week - Challenge members to perform a random act of kindness for a fellow member during the week, or have members share stories of acts of kindness that went humorously wrong.

February 17th: Do a Grouch a favour day - apply the above to the club grouches.

February 20th: World Day of Social Justice - Have some members share the world or local injustice issues that most appall them.

February 21st: International Mother Language Day - Have meeting items introduced in the mother language of migrant members.

February 23rd: Rotary's Birthday - Have a birthday theme and decorations for the meeting, or just a cake.

13. HEADS AND TAILS SEGMENT

You need two differnt coins and two members to flip the coins – one each. Every participant has to stand and take up one of three positions: Heads – both hands on their head; Tails – both hands on their backside; Odds – one hand on their head and one on their backside.Once participants have taken up their positions, the two "coin flippers" toss their coins into the air,catch them with one hand and slap them onto the back of their other hand to reveal either a "head" or a "tail" They call out one of three possible combinations: Two tails = "Tails"; two heads = "heads", onehead and one tail = "odds". Participants who have taken up the corresponding position to the coin toss remain standing. All others sit down. Those remaining standing have to take up one of three positions again and coins are tossed again. The game continues until either one player remains standing and wins a small prize, or all have been eliminated.

14. COLOR ELIMINATION SEGMENT

Set Up: You will need a set of cards or pieces of paper with one common color written on each, and a container e.g. a hat or small box. Suggested colors: black, white, red, green, blue, yellow, grey, brown, orange, pink, cream, purple. Alternatively have a set of 12 colored pencils or colored markers. Every participant stands and the game master takes out one of the colored cards or pencils and announces the color. e.g. grey. Everyone wearing any item of clothing or underclothing matching any variation of the announced color can remain standing – all others must sit down and are "out" of the game. The game master then produces another color e.g. blue. Those wearing any form of this color can remain standing. Further colors are produced until one person remains standing and wins a small prize, or all have been eliminated.

An alternative to this game is to have participants sit down if they are wearing the announced color.

15. MONTE CARLO SEGMENT

Set Up: You need a pack of cards. The Ace of each suit is "blue-tacked" (sticky putty) or pinned in a different corner of the room or meeting area. Participants choose to gather in one of the four corners near its card. One member is asked to select a card at random from the remainder of the pack and depending on the suite that is chosen, the group standing beside the ace of that suite must sit down. The remaining members then re-allocate themselves around the room and the same process of elimination continues until there are only four members left. They must select one of the suites each and this time, the suite that is chosen determines the winner.

16. SPIN THE BOTTLE SEGMENT

An elimination game similar to Monte Carlo but this time, members arrange themselves in four corners of the meeting area and a bottle is spun on the floor or a table. Once it comes to a stop, the bottle will point to a corner of the room and members standing in that corner will be eliminated from the game.

Fun Ideas for Whole Rotary Club Meetings or Meeting Themes

HOW TO USE THESE IDEAS

Each of these events could be ran in place of a standard meeting or tried as combined event with some nearby Rotary Clubs. One of these events could be run each month, or once a quarter or whenever.

1. "ROTARIANS GOT TALENT" OR "ROTARY IDOL"

Use the diverse talents of your members to conduct an event of entertainment

2. HAVE SPOUSES/ PARTNERS RUN THE MEETING

Try a meeting where all the leadership roles are conducted by partners or spouses of current Rotarians e.g. one could go the Sergeant, one could go the Chair etc.

3. HAVE MEMBERS' CHILDREN RUN THE MEETING

Use a group of capable older children (Grades 6 to 10) of members or grandchildren of members to conduct the meeting as a way of celebrating the "Family of Rotary". The selected children should be invited to attend a few meetings beforehand to get an idea of what goes on, and they would need a little coaching, but many young people from the ages of 12 to 16 can satisfactorily conduct a meeting.

4. HAVE A PRESIDENT FROM ANOTHER CLUB RUN THE MEETING

Invite a president from another club to run the meeting using the rituals common to the visiting President's club.

5.   ROTARACTORS OR INTERACTERS RUN THE MEETING

Have members from nearby Rotaract or Interact clubs to run the meeting

6.   RUN THE MEETING BACKWARDS

Start with the farewell, and work through the usual meeting procedure in reverse, and finish by welcoming everyone to the meeting.

7.   "SPEED DATING" FOR PROFESSIONAL CONTACTS.

Set up a night where you invite professionals from your town to join your members in a "Speed-Networking" experience. All participants are given a sequence of numbers relating to table numbers and after each course of a multi course meal or after

8.   CASINO NIGHT—JUST FOR FUN

Use the resources of members to set up a fun Casino in the meeting area. Have a variety of games e.g. Blackjack, Roulette, Big Spinning Wheel, Show Poker etc. and provide participants with a supply of chips they can use to participate in the games. The player with the most chips at the end of the night wins a prize. Alternatively, have an event playing just one type of game e.g. a poker tournament.

9.   AS A ROTARIAN, IF YOU COULD DO THINGS DIFFERENTLY AT TODAY'S MEETING, HOW WOULD YOU DO THEM?

Members take it in turns to run a meeting the way they would like it to be run. They can introduce new segments and run things in their own order.

10. INVITE A LOCAL WINERY TO CONDUCT A WINE TASTING AT YOUR CLUB VENUE – OR ALTERNATIVELY, TRANSPORT YOUR MEMBERS BY BUS TO A NEARBY WINERY AND HAVE YOUR MEETING THERE.

11. REUNION MEETINGS—BRING BACK PAST ROTARIANS

Invite all past members of your club to come back and see how the club has changed (or not).

12. THANK YOU MEETINGS—TO THANK PEOPLE WHO HAVE HELPED THE CLUB

Invite all people who have helped the club to come to a "Thank You" dinner where you can show some photos and movies of their work and present them with a "Thank You" certificate.

13. ROTARY CLUB COOK OFF

Get 3 or 4 of your best club member "chefs" to cook up their favorite dishes and explain how they do it everyone samples the results.

14. CHRISTMAS PARTY

*(From the Black Creek Lions Club) At the Christmas party (again with spouses), we asked each member/guest to bring a gift - $5 value. Everyone attending selected a number from the hat. The President drew the first number. The person with that number (Eugene) selected any gift he wanted and opened it. The President drew another number. That person (John) could take the gift away from Eugene or select from the table. Another number was drawn and that person (Julie) could take the gift from Eugene or John or from the table. The process continues. People went home with a wide variety of gifts nice, funny, naughty, and silly.

15. BARBEQUES OR PICNICS OR BYO & SHARE MEAL AT THE HOME OF A MEMBER OR PICNIC IN THE PARK

16. PROGRESSIVE DINNER OR MYSTERY DINNER OR GUESS WHO'S COMING TO DINNER

Conduct a dinner where the group moves from one venue to the next for each course. Or, load every member onto a bus and head off to a mystery restaurant for dinner. Or have a series of dinners where groups of 5 or 6 members and partners are invited to a location for dinner (or supper, or drinks) without them knowing who else will be at the event. Mix up people who don't usually sit together at meetings etc.

17. SPORTS CHALLENGE NIGHTS WITH NEARBY OR OTHER GROUP CLUBS E.G. BOWLS, TEN PIN BOWLS, MINI GOLF, CLAY TARGET SHOOTING

Have a fun night with a nearby club, (even from a different service organization) where members play sports in teams comprising members from different clubs.

18. CAR OBSERVATION CRUISE IN THE AREA (DON'T CALL IT A RALLY OR RACE— SEE INSURANCE EXCLUSIONS) OR A FOUR WHEEL DRIVE TRIP

Basically, a fun drive with some fun requirements to be met along the way.

Maybe have a secret "recommended safe time" to complete the journey and the winner is the vehicle closest to the recommended safe time.

19. EASY WALKS WITH A PICNIC AT THE END

20. DVD MOVIE WATCHING NIGHT AT A HOME OR MEETING AREA COMPLETE WITH POPCORN ETC.

21. CARD NIGHT E.G. 500, CRIBBAGE, CRAZY WHIST, TEXAS POKER USING TOKENS INSTEAD OF $$$

22. VALENTINE'S DAY OR ANY OTHER SPECIAL DAY DINNER

23. MUSIC NIGHTS—SING-A-LONGS, AND/OR MUSIC TRIVIA QUIZ FOR ALL AGES, MAYBE KARAOKE SINGING?

24. "HOST A MURDER" NIGHT

Use some of the commercial "Host a Murder" sets to have a dinner whilst playing one of the games.

25. COCKTAIL PARTY AT A MEMBER'S HOME

26. FANCY DRESS NIGHTS—USING THEMES AND MUSIC AND DECORATIONS

E.g. A Blue (or any other color) night, Halloween night, Glitzy Night, Roaring 20's night, 60's or 70's Psychedelic night etc.

27. NEW & OLD BOARD GAMES NIGHTS E.G. MONOPOLY, CLUE, DO, BALDERDASH, SCATTERGORIES, ETC.

Have a range of board games available.

28. DANCE PARTY THROUGH THE AGES AND CULTURES

Play dance music from different countries and eras for all ages—maybe free lessons?

Public Relations and Awareness

Public Relations Pointers

Much is said about the need for good PR and for Clubs to find ways to promote the work they do in their local communities and across the world.

Where do you start to create a PR message to share with our target audience?

You can use banners and create billboards. You can wear bright colourful shirts when out and about at work in your local community and you can hand out brochures when cooking up sausages on your Club BBQ. You can write press releases and send them to your local newspapers – some regional areas have much more success than the city based Clubs where money is needed to pay for any information to be printed.

You can use your Club websites to promote yourselves and you can make videos and upload them to YouTube. You can create social media pages to reach out to the widest possible audience. There are many ways to let your community about the work of your club and, more importantly, invite them to join in the work you do.

Start at the Beginning

Create a PR plan for your Club and request a budget from the Board. Set some goals around what you want to achieve, from a PR perspective. If the role of PR is not represented on your Club Board, then it needs to be.

Think about the projects and events your Club will be involved in and the charities your Club will be supporting. Plan to use these activities as a basis for promoting your Club.

Do you have someone in your Club who loves taking photos or a Club Photographer as a member of your PR team? Good PR is made better with quality photographs, especially if you are using social media to promote your Club.

Use Social Media

The best thing about Social Media is that it's free! You can easily create a Facebook Page to share information about your Club.

Some ideas for Facebook Administrators

- Create your page as an organization and NOT as a person – you need LIKERS rather than FRIENDS.
- Always have at least two people in your Club with administrator status to share the posting. Make sure that if one person is not able to maintain the page, the other has access and will do posts.
- Let pictures tell your story. A few words and powerful images will have more impact than lengthy prose.
- Post regularly – at least once or twice a week. Social media is an immediate communication channel and your followers will disappear if you don't regularly give them something to LIKE.

Facebook does not deliver every post to all LIKERS of your page. If you want to increase the VIEWINGS, LIKES and COMMENTS around your posts you need to BOOST. This involves paying a small amount to transform the numbers of people who see your post from perhaps 100 to several thousand.

Resources

Use the staff and websites of your organization for guidelines on

- Logo use
- Fonts & Colors
- Suggested graphics
- Sample posts, templates, premade ads for TV and radio
- Guides for websites, social media, ideas, messaging, etc.

Public Relations Tips and Tricks for Your Organization

- Follow up with customers through email.
- Harness power of social media.
- Build brand through blogging.
- Be a part of the conversation online.
- Maintain relationships with journalists.

Marketing is a dirty word for many community-based nonprofits. Nonprofits, with purer motivations and lofty goals, tend to spurn a lot of traditional public relations strategies. But that's old thinking. To win the war of public opinion, attract new activists, and educate potential investors, nonprofits are learning that they need to use "free" or "earned" media in a new and savvier way.

Here are tips to getting your nonprofit the publicity it deserves.

1. **Put yourself in a reader's shoes.**
   a. Try to think like the average newspaper reader — follow opinion polls, search through the paper for stories, determine what editors think their readers find important. Editors are your audience, because they'll be deciding if your story runs.

2. **Know what part your nonprofit plays in the larger community.**

3. **Articulate the message.**
   a. See if you can articulate your nonprofit's event or announcement in words a regular reader will care about. In other words, be sure what you're doing IS newsworthy.

4. **Build a relationship with your press contacts.**
   a. Whether you're ready to pitch a news story or an upcoming event, a program or a report, a legal action or a new partnership– it's time to put faces, or at least voices, to your press contacts. Get to know editors and reporters. If one isn't in when you call, you should always have a back-up. Assign a press spokesperson to handle all media inquiries.
   b. When your nonprofit has a story to pitch, have your press spokesperson call the reporter and give him or her a brief summary. If there's interest, the reporter will ask for more information. (He or she then has to pitch it to the editor.)

5. **Be available.**
   a. If you aren't the press spokesperson for your nonprofit, make sure that person is available to be interviewed and quoted. Prepare your press spokesperson for some of the questions you can anticipate. After the story runs, call the reporter and offer feedback, especially if it's positive.

Nonprofit public relations involves an entire strategy of building name-recognition, developing an action program that is relevant to the larger public, and following through on relationships with your press contacts. These steps are only your first on the road to getting publicity for your nonprofit, but with persistence, nonprofits can become adept at the world of public relations.

LEADERSHIP ISN'T WHAT IT IS CRACKED UP TO BE!

Please don't despair – Being President of your club is VERY rewarding.

President Elect Year

Congratulations on being selected/elected as President-Elect for your club. There are many things to think about, attend and plan. Use this guide to make the planning less stressful and more organized.

Topics to consider for this time period. Hopefully you will hape a full club year as Elect, but many do not. The timelines have been condensed to 6 months to accommodate for this.

- Trainings
- Member information
- Budget
- Officers and Chairpersons
- Goals and Objectives
- Strategic Plan
- Club Traditions and Activities

President Elect Responsibilities

- Consult the club president on decisions affecting the club
- Appoint committee chairs for your year
- Encourage incoming club officers to attend district training assembly
- Serve as a director of your club's board, performing responsibilities prescribed by the president or the board
- Review the Club President's Manual and attend the President-Elect Training events provided by the District
- Review your club's long-range strategic goals and ensure that the club's strategic plan is reviewed or updated in readiness for your year – every committee should have its own comprehensive list of strategic goals.
- Attend your President-Elect Training Seminar and District Assembly - Make yourself known to your assistant governor at these events
- Encourage all club leaders to attend the District Assembly
- Appoint committee chairs and members to committees (ideally to the same committee for two or three years to maintain continuity)
- Attend the District Conference

January	
Make sure you have registered on RI's website - i.e. My Rotary. Practice using this website and explore what it offers and how to access things. A great resource and it is being consistently enhanced by RI to make it easier to use.	
Become familiar with your District website. It has many useful documents.	
The new Presidental theme for your year and Citation are announced at the International Assembly for District Governor-Elects. Find out what is announced, as it will help guide you in your planning.	
If you haven't already done so, approach people to be on your Board, and work with them to structure their committees.	
President, Secretary and Treasurer for your year of service needs to be reported to your club, district and RI as soon as possible. Follow their guidelines and procedures for sharing this information.	
Find out when President Elect Training Seminar (PETS) for your area is held and REGISTER.	

Notes:

February	
If you haven't already done so, approach people to be on your Board, and work with them to structure their committees.	
Review the club's constitution and by-laws.	
Attend President Elect Training Seminar (PETS) for your area.	
Make sure you have registered on RI's website - i.e. My Rotary. Practice using this website and explore what it offers and how to access things. A great resource and it is being consistently enhanced by RI to make it easier to use.	
Become familiar with your District website. It has many useful documents.	
Attend any Trainings or meetings your District or zone may be holding.	
Visit other clubs in your area and introduce yourself to their President-Elect. Plan joint projects and how you could together.	

Notes:

March	
If you haven't already done so, approach people to be on your Board, and work with them to structure their committees.	
Make sure you have registered on RI's website - i.e. My Rotary. Practice using this website and explore what it offers and how to access things. A great resource and it is being consistently enhanced by RI to make it easier to use.	
Become familiar with your District website. It has many useful documents.	
Attend the District Assembly together with as many of your Board as possible.	

Notes:

April	
If you haven't already done so, approach people to be on your Board, and work with them to structure their committees.	
Review the club's constitution and by-laws.	
Locate the following: • The club's EIN • The club's Incorporation number, if incorporated. • The club's RI number • A copy of the club's constitution and bylaws updated after the latest Council on Legislation	
Attend the District Assembly together with as many of your Board as possible.	
Organize a planning meeting for your Board • what will be each person's responsibilities; • what will be carrying over from the current year; • what strengths does the club have to build on; • where could improvements be made; • what projects will you focus on; • will you want to apply for a District Grant from the Foundation. (Information about District Grant application process can be found on the District website.)	

Notes:

May	
Create a club calendar with board meetings and club assemblies in place. Use the Planning pages at the end of this book.	
Decide how you will organize and run your meetings. An agenda for club meetings and one for board meetings is essential.	
See that the outgoing and incoming treasurers are working on a club budget for your year - what will you allocate to which programs. Discuss and review club fees.	
Check that you know the following: • The location of the club's Charter • How to look up something in the Manual of Procedure (Go to www.rotary.org; click on My Rotary; Click on Learning and Reference; Click on Documents.)	
DDF Grants final report from current year is due on May 31. (May be different in your area - check to make sure any reporting is complete.)	
Coordinate with the outgoing President about the Changeover/ Installation function - what will be your role, what will you have to do.	
Check with the outgoing secretary that membership details are up to date and accurate as at 31 May on the RI website, as this will determine the dues that will be paid in July. (The amount cannot be changed!)	
Set a date for your Changeover/Installation and inform the club members and any District staff, as needed.	

June	
Have a combined Board meeting with the out-going Board to discuss the hand-over of materials and projects, etc.	
Make sure the treasurer has arranged to change the signatures at the bank - will probably need to take a copy of the minutes of the Board meeting appointing the new club leadership (President & Secretary).	
Take part in the Club Changeover/Installation as planned.	
Have your Board assist you to enter all your goals onto Rotary Club Central. **This approach will avoid the need to fill out any planning documents for the DG's visit. More importantly, it will help make your year as President much easier.**	
Think about how you might accommodate for the following important ways to build a strong and caring club by remembering the welfare of your members ... people who have no particular role on your board may be given responsibilities here: • Establish a system to follow up and stay in touch with club members who have missed recent meetings to make sure everything is OK; • Invite members to bring their partners and/or children/other family members to a club meeting or club event on a regular basis; • Acknowledge the importance of Rotarians' families and their contribution to our club's success; • Re-connect with people who have benefited from Rotary in the past: Scholarship recipients, short or long-term exchange students, RYLA participants, contest winners, service project participants, and anyone who has been touched by the club in the past; • Find ways to honor or otherwise recognize Rotary club members throughout our community;	

Notes:

Tools - What You Can Do On Rotary.org

- See your club snapshot and reports
- Perform administrative tasks:
  - Confirm officers have migrated upward from your partner software
  - Pay your club invoice
  - Generate Foundation and membership reports
  - Submit nominations for awards
  - Get club forms

Rotary Club Central

- Enter club goals and achievements in membership, service, and giving
- Review and adjust goals
- View club trends and reports

Rotary Brand Center

- Download Rotary logos
- Create a club logo and stationery
- Find templates for business cards, newsletters, and fliers

Rotary Ideas

- Find resources for your projects:
  - Partners
  - Volunteers
  - Material contributions
  - Direct online financial contributions

Rotary Showcase

- Share photos and videos from successful projects
- Report the project's contribution to Rotary's global impact

Learning Center

- Find training by role or by topic
- Take courses at your own pace, on topics that interest you

Discussion Groups

- Find others who share your interests
- Meet other Rotary officers
- Start a new discussion group
- Learn from diverse global perspectives

Notes / Comments / Ideas Gathered at PETS

Notes / Comments / Ideas Gathered at PETS

Notes / Comments / Ideas Gathered at PETS

Contacts Gathered at PETS

Write or staple business cards of contacts made with fellow President-Elects, possible speakers, Resources for assistance.

Club Officers and Directors for your Year as President		
Name	Office	Yes/No

Preparing for Your Meetings as President

As President you will be handling many meetings throughout the year. The following guidelines will assist in planning an agenda and running any type of meeting.

Structure of a Typical Agenda

The typical written agenda has a heading of identifying information. Other parts of the agenda appear like an outline using Roman numerals to identify board items for discussion.

Heading

The heading of the agenda should state the name and address of the organization. It should also include the date, time, and location of the meeting.

Call to Order

The first order of business is for the chair to announce the call to order, along with the time. The secretary enters the time of the call to order in the minutes. After the meeting is called to order, the board chair may make welcoming remarks, ask for introductions, or read the organization's mission and vision statements.

Changes to the Agenda

The second order of business is for the chair to ask for changes to the agenda. Additions and deletions to the agenda will be made at this time. Having no changes, the agenda moves to approving the prior meeting's minutes.

Approval of Minutes

The third item on the agenda should list "Approval of Minutes" along with the date of the most recent meeting. In most cases, board members should have received a copy of the minutes prior to the meeting. If they have not contacted the secretary prior to the meeting with corrections or changes to the minutes, they have to opportunity to make them during this item on the agenda.

Board members have an ethical and legal responsibility to make sure that the recording of the minutes accurately reflect the board's business.

Reports

The fourth item on the agenda is the reports. The first report should be a financial report from the Treasurer. It should include, at a minimum, a balance sheet of all accounts, a budget summary, and a request for approval any bills to be paid. Board members may request more information at any time. Board policy will determine if this needs to be approved by a motion and vote.

Subsequent reports may be given by committee chairs.

Old Business

Items should include past business items that are unresolved, need further discussion, or require a board vote. Items may be tabled or referred to committee for further exploration.

New Business

Board members should have a discussion about new business items and identify a plan to take action. This may include tabling them, delaying action to a future date, or referring them to a committee.

Comments, Announcements, and Other Business

At this point in the agenda, members may make announcements, such as offering congratulations or condolences, or make other special announcements. Any other business may be brought up at this time, for example, items that may need to be added to the next meeting's agenda.

Adjournment

This is a formal closing of the meeting by the board chair. He should state the time that the meeting closed, so that the secretary may including it in the board minutes. The date of the next meeting should follow the adjournment item, so that board members will be reminded to put it on their calendars.

On the
Agenda

Parliamentary Procedure for Meetings

Robert's Rules of Order is the standard for facilitating discussions and group decision-making. Copies of the rules are available at most bookstores. Although they may seem long and involved, having an agreed- upon set of rules makes meetings run easier. Robert's Rules will help your group have better meetings, not make them more difficult. Your group is free to modify them or find another suitable process that encourages fairness and participation, unless your bylaws state otherwise.

Here are the basic elements of Robert's Rules, used by most organizations:

1. **Motion:** To introduce a new piece of business or propose a decision or action, a motion must be made by a group member ("I move that......") A second motion must then also be made (raise your hand and say, "I second it.") After limited discussion the group then votes on the motion. A majority vote is required for the motion to pass (or quorum as specified in your bylaws.)

2. **Postpone Indefinitely:** This tactic is used to kill a motion. When passed, the motion cannot be reintroduced at that meeting. It may be brought up again at a later date. This is made as a motion ("I move to postpone indefinitely..."). A second is required. A majority vote is required to postpone the motion under consideration.

3. **Amend:** This is the process used to change a motion under consideration. Perhaps you like the idea proposed but not exactly as offered. Raise your hand and make the following motion: "I move to amend the motion on the floor." This also requires a second. After the motion to amend is seconded, a majority vote is needed to decide whether the amendment is accepted. Then a vote is taken on the amended motion. In some organizations, a "friendly amendment" is made. If the person who made the original motion agrees with the suggested changes, the amended motion may be voted on without a separate vote to approve the amendment.

4. **Commit:** This is used to place a motion in committee. It requires a second. A majority vote must rule to carry it. At the next meeting the committee is required to prepare a report on the motion committed. If an appropriate committee exists, the motion goes to that committee. If not, a new committee is established.

5. **Question:** To end a debate immediately, the question is called (say "I call the question") and needs a second. A vote is held immediately (no further discussion is allowed). A two-thirds vote is required for passage. If it is passed, the motion on the floor is voted on immediately.

6. **Table:** To table a discussion is to lay aside the business at hand in such a manner that it will be considered later in the meeting or at another time ("I make a motion to table this discussion until the next meeting. In the meantime, we will get more information, so we can better discuss the issue.") A second is needed and a majority vote required to table the item being discussed.

7. **Adjourn:** A motion is made to end the meeting. A second motion is required. A majority vote is then required for the meeting to be adjourned (ended).

Note: If more than one motion is proposed, the most recent takes precedence over the ones preceding it. For example if #6, a motion to table the discussion, is proposed, it must be voted on before #3, a motion to amend, can be decided.

In a smaller meeting, like a committee or board meeting, often only four motions are used:

- To introduce (motion.)
- To change a motion (amend.)
- To adopt (accept a report without discussion.)
- To adjourn (end the meeting.)

Remember, these processes are designed to ensure that everyone has a chance to participate and to share ideas in an orderly manner. Parliamentary procedure should not be used to prevent discussion of important issues.

Board and committee chairpersons and other leaders may want to get some training in meeting facilitation and in using parliamentary procedure. Additional information on meeting processes, dealing with difficult people, and using Robert's Rules is available.

Tips in Parliamentary Procedure

The following summary will help you determine when to use the actions described in Robert's Rules.

- A main motion must be moved, seconded, and stated by the chair before it can be discussed.
- If you want to move, second, or speak to a motion, *stand and address the chair.*
- If you approve the motion as is, *vote for it.*
- If you disapprove the motion, *vote against it.*
- If you approve the idea of the motion but want to change it, amend it or

submit a substitute for it.

- If you want advice or information to help you make your decision, *move to refer the motion to an appropriate quorum or committee with instructions to report back.*
- If you feel they can handle it better than the assembly, *move to refer the motion to a quorum or committee with power to act.*
- If you feel that there the pending question(s) should be delayed so more urgent business can be considered, *move to lay the motion on the table.*
- If you want time to think the motion over, move that consideration be deferred to a certain time.
- If you think that further discussion is unnecessary, *move the previous question.*
- If you think that the assembly should give further consideration to a motion referred to a quorum or committee, *move the motion be recalled.*
- If you think that the assembly should give further consideration to a matter already voted upon, *move that it be reconsidered.*
- If you do not agree with a decision rendered by the chair, *appeal the decision to the assembly.*
- If you think that a matter introduced is not germane to the matter at hand, *a point of order may be raised.*
- If you think that too much time is being consumed by speakers, *you can move a time limit on such speeches.*
- If a motion has several parts, and you wish to vote differently on these parts, *move to divide the motion.*

IN THE MEETING

TO INTRODUCE A MOTION:

Stand when no one else has the floor.

Address the Chair by the proper title.

Wait until the chair recognizes you.

- Now that you have the floor and can proceed with your motion say "I move that...," state your motion clearly and sit down.
- Another member may second your motion. A second merely implies that the seconder agrees that the motion should come before the assembly and not that he/she is in favor of the motion.
- If there is no second, the Chair says, "The motion is not before you at this time." The motion is not lost, as there has been no vote taken.
- If there is a second, the Chair states the question by saying "It has been moved and seconded that ... (state the motion). . ., is there any

discussion?"

DEBATE OR DISCUSSING THE MOTION:

- The member who made the motion is entitled to speak first.
- Every member has the right to speak in debate.
- The Chair should alternate between those "for" the motion and those "against" the motion.
- The discussion should be related to the pending motion.
- Avoid using a person's name in debate.
- All questions should be directed to the Chair.
- Unless there is a special rule providing otherwise, a member is limited to speak once to a motion.
- Asking a question or a brief suggestion is not counted in debate.
- A person may speak a second time in debate with the assembly's permission.

VOTING ON A MOTION:

- Before a vote is taken, the Chair puts the question by saying "Those in favor of the motion that ... (repeat the motion)... say "Aye." Those opposed say "No." Wait, then say "The motion is carried," or "The motion is lost."
- Some motions require a 2/3 vote. A 2/3 vote is obtained by standing
- If a member is in doubt about the vote, he may call out "division." A division is a demand for a standing vote.
- A majority vote is more than half of the votes cast by persons legally entitled to vote.
- A 2/3 vote means at least 2/3 of the votes cast by persons legally entitled to vote.
- A tie vote is a lost vote, since it is not a majority.

Your Year as President

The following pages provide space and additional information to complete the responsibilites listed above.

- District Activities and Events
- Service Projects
- Membership Activities for Growth & Retention
- Activities and Fundraisers
- Public Relations and Awareness
- Club Meetings

Unexpected Events and Emergencies

Although they are rare, unfortunately emergency situations do occasionally arise. Preparation for any possibility is an essential part of planning for the continued operation and life of an organization. How the community and the media perceive that the emergency was handled will have a direct impact on the organization. The following guidelines outline how to prepare in advance for a possible emergency, the individuals to contact should an emergency occur, and the steps to follow during an emergency.

Because all emergencies/disasters begin locally, it is the responsibility of individual Rotary clubs to develop plans within the guidelines of the District Disaster Plan. The club president and the club board of directors are responsible for the club plan. The club president is responsible for coordinating the efforts of the club with local emergency management organizations as long as the event requiring a response remains local. In the event a Rotary Club or a group of clubs within a locale are asked by local emergency management authorities to assist, the club(s) involved should notify the District Governor or a member of the District Disaster Relief Committee.

The Objectives and Roles of a President

1. Provide leadership that enables the club to sustain or increase its membership base, implement successful projects that address the needs of their community and communities in other countries and support the Rotary Foundation through both program participation and financial contributions
2. Develop leaders capable of serving in Rotary beyond the club level

Specific Responsibilities

- Ensure you are registered for My Rotary at www.rotary.org to obtain your club's administrative data from RI. You should also have logins for any club or district software used.

- Ensure the club secretary has registered for My Rotary in order to keep membership and club data up- to-date. Secretary should also have logins for any club or district software used.
- Implement and continually evaluate your club's goals for your year of office, assuring that all club members are involved and informed
- Ensure that each committee has defined goals for the year
- Encourage communication between club and district committee chairs
- Conduct periodic reviews of all committee activities, goals, and expenditures
- Preside at all meetings of the club Board ensuring that all meetings are carefully planned and that important information is communicated to club members
- Provide regular fellowship opportunities for members
- Prepare for, and encourage member participation in club and district meetings
- Plan for all monthly board meetings
- Attend and ensure club representation at the District Conference and other district meetings
- Attend District Assembly and hold an information session immediately following the District Assembly to pass on relevant information to members
- Work with your club and district leaders to develop, approve, and monitor the club budget while working closely with the club treasurer
- Work with district leadership to achieve club and district goals using information and resources from the district, RI Secretariat, and the RI Web site
- Ensure continuity in leadership and service projects
- Submit a comprehensive annual report to your club on its status in June, before leaving office.
- Confer with your successor before leaving office to ensure a smooth transition especially with regard to what is involved in the Changeover/ Installtion.
- Arrange for a joint meeting of the incoming board with the outgoing board of directors Use the Club President's Monthly Checklist when planning your year as president and reviewing your responsibilities as president elect and president.

Your Activities and Events

Use the following pages and lists to complete and remind you of events and activities throughout your year.

District Activities and Events I will attend	

Service Projects I want to plan & Implement

Membership Acitivities for Growth & Retention	

Fundraisers during this year	

How will the Club publicize what we are doing?

Club Meeting Planner/Memory Pages

You will want to remember your year - maybe not all the little bits, but the big bits - YES!

Use the following pages to guide you through your year and plan effectively and completely.

July - New Leadership	
• Hold a Club Assembly for discussion of club matters.	
• Inform Club Members of this year's yearly/half yearly fees and that they are due 31st July and 31st January	
• By 31 July: Ensure Secretary / Treasurer has received the Club Invoice and has arranged payment. Pay District Dues to District Treasurer.	
• Feature the new Presidential/District theme in your meetings: _____ . Discuss what it means to each member, and how it can be put into practice in your club.	
• Introduce the new RI President to your club - who is (s)he and what does (s)he aim to achieve?	
• Outline the Presidential Citation for this year to your members. How can you incorporate these goals into your planning for the year? A copy of the Presidential Citation was provided at PETS. Do the same for any District awards, if applicable.	
• Hold a board meeting	

JULY IS

NEW LEADERSHIP MONTH

"To improve is to change; to be perfect is to change often. "
Winston Churchill

Rotary

www.rotary.org

Meeting Date _____

Program/Speaker _____

Invocation _____

Pledge _____

4 Way Test _____

Other Club Tradition _____

Other Club Tradition _____

Other Club Tradition _____

Other Club Tradition _____

Guests: _____

_____

_____

_____

Notes/Comments/Special Moments:

Meeting Date _____

Program/Speaker _____

Invocation _____

Pledge _____

4 Way Test _____

Other Club Tradition _____

Other Club Tradition _____

Other Club Tradition _____

Other Club Tradition _____

Guests: _____

_____

_____

_____

Notes/Comments/Special Moments:

Meeting Date _____

Program/Speaker _____

Invocation _____

Pledge _____

4 Way Test _____

Other Club Tradition _____

Other Club Tradition _____

Other Club Tradition _____

Other Club Tradition _____

Guests: _____

_____

_____

_____

Notes/Comments/Special Moments:

Meeting Date _____

Program/Speaker _____

Invocation _____

Pledge _____

4 Way Test _____

Other Club Tradition _____

Other Club Tradition _____

Other Club Tradition _____

Other Club Tradition _____

Guests: _____

_____

_____

_____

Notes/Comments/Special Moments:

Meeting Date _____

Program/Speaker _____

Invocation _____

Pledge _____

4 Way Test _____

Other Club Tradition _____

Other Club Tradition _____

Other Club Tradition _____

Other Club Tradition _____

Guests: _____

_____

_____

_____

Notes/Comments/Special Moments:

August - Membership and Extension Month

Arrange for the Club's finances to be audited by an approved person

Some ideas for Membership Month

- Take turns inviting guests. Members should take turns inviting prospective members to club meetings. At least one member should be expected to bring a guest every week. This effort could be conducted in alphabetical order, based on the members' first or last names.   This consistent approach to growth helps get members in the habit of identifying prospects and asking them to join.
- Organize teams. Organize teams of 4 or 5 club members. The goal of each team is to recruit one new member within 3 or 4 months. Each team needs one member who is active in the community, one knowledgeable about Rotary and one who is prepared to make cold calls to sell Rotary.
- Go public. Ask one or two members to work on a public relations campaign, sending news releases about your club to local newspapers, radio and TV stations or put up a billboard or use truck ads to promote Rotary. Make sure to include a contact phone number, e-mail address or web site.
- Feature great programs. Once you succeed in getting guests to a meeting, make sure they like what they see. Organize interesting club meeting programs that will make those guests want to come back for more.
- Educate members. The more your members know about Rotary, the better they will be able to sell Rotary to prospective members. Make sure your club meetings feature regular Rotary education segments. One program every month should be on a Rotary topic.
- Start a speaker's bureau. Just as outside speakers promote their causes to your club, your members can visit other organizations and talk about how they are helping the community, eradicating polio and sending more than 7,000 Youth Exchange Students around the world. While they're speaking, they can hand out club your club brochure.

- Make the most of your service projects. Every time your club conducts a service project (which is hopefully often); promote Rotary to those you're serving. If your club invites the parents of scholarship winners or outgoing Youth Exchange Students to club meetings, give them information on Rotary and encourage them to join. If your club makes a contribution to a local charity, ask the staff members to visit your club.
- Learn from others. Scan your district bulletin and other publications for news of clubs that have recently grown. Pay those clubs a visit and find out how they increased their membership. Observe how they handle their meetings and welcome guests to the group.
- Sing your praises. Don't be bashful about your involvement in Rotary. Whether at work or at play, talk up Rotary to those around you. You never know when you might strike a responsive cord with someone just waiting to get involved. Always wear your Rotary pin.
- Increase your circulation. Does your club send a bulletin to members before every meeting? Why not increase its circulation? Send copies to prospective members, to media professionals and to former members. Add a personal note on each, inviting the recipient to attend the next meeting.
- Roll out the welcome mat. Whenever guests come to a meeting, make them feel right at home. Encourage your members to introduce themselves and talk up the club. Many clubs assign one or two long-time members to accompany the prospect and make sure he or she gets a good introduction to your Rotary Club. First impressions are important.
- Put prospects to work. If your club is planning an upcoming service project, ask several prospective members to get involved. Why wait until they join the club? Perhaps hands-on involvement in a service project may be just the thing to prod some good prospects into making a commitment to Rotary.
- Plan a fun event and invite prospective members.

Hold a board meeting

AUGUST IS
CLUB
MEMBERSHIP
& NEW CLUB
DEVELOPMENT
MONTH
"Rotary's strength lies in the sincerity of purpose of its members."
Estes Snedecor, Rotary Club of Portland, Oregon - 1921 Rotary Convention
Rotary
EACH ROTARIAN:
REACH ONE, KEEP ONE
www.rotary.org

Notes:

Meeting Date _____

Program/Speaker _____

Invocation _____

Pledge _____

4 Way Test _____

Other Club Tradition _____

Other Club Tradition _____

Other Club Tradition _____

Other Club Tradition _____

Guests: _____

_____

_____

_____

Notes/Comments/Special Moments:

Meeting Date _____

Program/Speaker _____

Invocation _____

Pledge _____

4 Way Test _____

Other Club Tradition _____

Other Club Tradition _____

Other Club Tradition _____

Other Club Tradition _____

Guests: _____

_____

_____

_____

Notes/Comments/Special Moments:

Meeting Date _____

Program/Speaker _____

Invocation _____

Pledge _____

4 Way Test _____

Other Club Tradition _____

Other Club Tradition _____

Other Club Tradition _____

Other Club Tradition _____

Guests: _____

_____

_____

_____

Notes/Comments/Special Moments:

Meeting Date _____

Program/Speaker _____

Invocation _____

Pledge _____

4 Way Test _____

Other Club Tradition _____

Other Club Tradition _____

Other Club Tradition _____

Other Club Tradition _____

Guests: _____

_____

_____

_____

Notes/Comments/Special Moments:

Meeting Date _____

Program/Speaker _____

Invocation _____

Pledge _____

4 Way Test _____

Other Club Tradition _____

Other Club Tradition _____

Other Club Tradition _____

Other Club Tradition _____

Guests: _____

_____

_____

_____

Notes/Comments/Special Moments:

September - Basic Education and Literacy Month

Include this information in your club bulletin this month and discuss it in a meeting.

The fifth Area of Focus for the Rotary Foundation Global Grants Program is Basic Education and Literacy. Below is a summary of how they see this best undertaken in developing countries:

Rotary supports activities and training to improve education for all children and literacy for children and adults.

Area of Focus Statement of Purpose and Goals

1. TRF enables Rotarians to ensure that all people have sustainable access to basic education and literacy by:

2. Involving the community to support programs that strengthen the capacity of communities to provide basic education and literacy to all;

3. Increasing adult literacy in communities;

4. Working to reduce gender disparity in education;

5. Supporting studies for career-minded professionals related to basic education and literacy.

Some ideas for Literacy Month:

- Make Literacy the focus for one of your meetings - invite a Literacy teacher as guest speaker
- Contribute an article to your local paper outlining some of Rotary's literacy projects
- Present a literacy award to a teacher, librarian, author, illustrator, bookseller, journalist, etc, and publicise the award(s).
- Approach your school to see if you can assist with reading programs
- Create a 'Shop or Swap' program where children can bring their books to swap with other books or buy.
- Buy some picture books or early readers and present them to your school (maybe $250). Publicize.
- Find out about the Dolly Parton's Imagination Library. You may be able to participate. www.imaginationlibrary.com

Hold a board meeting

Notes:

SEPTEMBER IS
BASIC EDUCATION
AND LITERACY
MONTH
"The more you read, the more things you will know. The more that you learn, the more places you'll go."
Dr. Seuss, "I Can Read With My Eyes Shut!"
Rotary
www.rotary.org

Meeting Date _____

Program/Speaker _____

Invocation _____

Pledge _____

4 Way Test _____

Other Club Tradition _____

Other Club Tradition _____

Other Club Tradition _____

Other Club Tradition _____

Guests: _____

_____

_____

_____

Notes/Comments/Special Moments:

Meeting Date _____

Program/Speaker _____

Invocation _____

Pledge _____

4 Way Test _____

Other Club Tradition _____

Other Club Tradition _____

Other Club Tradition _____

Other Club Tradition _____

Guests: _____

_____

_____

_____

Notes/Comments/Special Moments:

Meeting Date _____

Program/Speaker _____

Invocation _____

Pledge _____

4 Way Test _____

Other Club Tradition _____

Other Club Tradition _____

Other Club Tradition _____

Other Club Tradition _____

Guests: _____

_____

_____

_____

Notes/Comments/Special Moments:

Meeting Date _____

Program/Speaker _____

Invocation _____

Pledge _____

4 Way Test _____

Other Club Tradition _____

Other Club Tradition _____

Other Club Tradition _____

Other Club Tradition _____

Guests: _____

_____

_____

_____

Notes/Comments/Special Moments:

Meeting Date _____

Program/Speaker _____

Invocation _____

Pledge _____

4 Way Test _____

Other Club Tradition _____

Other Club Tradition _____

Other Club Tradition _____

Other Club Tradition _____

Guests: _____

_____

_____

_____

Notes/Comments/Special Moments:

October - Economic and Community Development Month

Include this information in your club bulletin this month, and discuss it in a meeting:

The sixth Area of Focus for the Rotary Foundation Global Grants Program is Economic and Community Development. Below is a summary of how they see this best undertaken in developing countries:

Rotary supports investments in people to create measurable and enduring economic improvement in their lives and communities.

Area of Focus Statement of Purpose and Goals

1. TRF enables Rotarians to invest in people by creating sustainable, measurable and long-term economic improvements in their communities and livelihoods by

2. Building the capacity of entrepreneurs, community leaders, local organizations, and community networks to support economic development in impoverished communities;

3. Developing opportunities for productive work;

4. Reducing poverty in underserved communities;

5. Supporting studies for career-minded professionals related to economic and community development.

Some Ideas for Economic and Community Development Month:

- Ask members to find articles The Rotarian that deal with this issue and discuss how your club might do something similar in the future;
- Find out what other clubs have achieved in your Rotary District to improve their local communities;
- Write an article for your local newspaper that outlines some of the ways your club has contributed to the welfare of your community over the years;
- Create a display of the above for your local library or other suitable venue;
- Hold a discussion in your club about what elements in your own local community could be improved using your members' skills, knowledge and service commitments. Use this discussion to draw up a list of potential local projects for the future;
- Update your club's goal achievements on **Rotary Club Central**.

Meeting Date _____

Program/Speaker _____

Invocation _____

Pledge _____

4 Way Test _____

Other Club Tradition _____

Other Club Tradition _____

Other Club Tradition _____

Other Club Tradition _____

Guests: _____

_____

_____

_____

Notes/Comments/Special Moments:

Meeting Date _____

Program/Speaker _____

Invocation _____

Pledge _____

4 Way Test _____

Other Club Tradition _____

Other Club Tradition _____

Other Club Tradition _____

Other Club Tradition _____

Guests: _____

_____

_____

_____

Notes/Comments/Special Moments:

Meeting Date _____

Program/Speaker _____

Invocation _____

Pledge _____

4 Way Test _____

Other Club Tradition _____

Other Club Tradition _____

Other Club Tradition _____

Other Club Tradition _____

Guests: _____

_____

_____

_____

Notes/Comments/Special Moments:

Meeting Date _____

Program/Speaker _____

Invocation _____

Pledge _____

4 Way Test _____

Other Club Tradition _____

Other Club Tradition _____

Other Club Tradition _____

Other Club Tradition _____

Guests: _____

_____

_____

_____

Notes/Comments/Special Moments:

Meeting Date _____

Program/Speaker _____

Invocation _____

Pledge _____

4 Way Test _____

Other Club Tradition _____

Other Club Tradition _____

Other Club Tradition _____

Other Club Tradition _____

Guests: _____

_____

_____

_____

Notes/Comments/Special Moments:

November - Rotary Foundation Month	
Some ideas for Rotary Foundation Month: • Have someone give a 3-5 minute talk each meeting about one of the Foundation programs - e.g. District Grants, Global Grants, PolioPlus campaign, Peace Scholarships. • Ask the District Rotary Foundation Chair to address your club about the Foundation. • Find out about a couple of the projects that have been funded in the current year. • Plan a local project for which you could apply for a District Grant next Rotary year. • Hold a fund-raising event for the Foundation, and to publicize the work of the Foundation. • Ask an alumnus to address the club about the value of their Foundation experience.	
Check that your club giving to the Foundation is on target - on Rotary Club Central.	
Give your members information about the Every Rotarian Every Year Program, and encourage every member to participate.	
Hold a board meeting	

Notes:

Meeting Date _____

Program/Speaker _____

Invocation _____

Pledge _____

4 Way Test _____

Other Club Tradition _____

Other Club Tradition _____

Other Club Tradition _____

Other Club Tradition _____

Guests: _____

_____

_____

_____

Notes/Comments/Special Moments:

Meeting Date _____

Program/Speaker _____

Invocation _____

Pledge _____

4 Way Test _____

Other Club Tradition _____

Other Club Tradition _____

Other Club Tradition _____

Other Club Tradition _____

Guests: _____

_____

_____

_____

Notes/Comments/Special Moments:

Meeting Date _____

Program/Speaker _____

Invocation _____

Pledge _____

4 Way Test _____

Other Club Tradition _____

Other Club Tradition _____

Other Club Tradition _____

Other Club Tradition _____

Guests: _____

_____

_____

_____

Notes/Comments/Special Moments:

Meeting Date _____

Program/Speaker _____

Invocation _____

Pledge _____

4 Way Test _____

Other Club Tradition _____

Other Club Tradition _____

Other Club Tradition _____

Other Club Tradition _____

Guests: _____

_____

_____

_____

Notes/Comments/Special Moments:

Meeting Date _____

Program/Speaker _____

Invocation _____

Pledge _____

4 Way Test _____

Other Club Tradition _____

Other Club Tradition _____

Other Club Tradition _____

Other Club Tradition _____

Guests: _____

_____

_____

_____

Notes/Comments/Special Moments:

December - Disease Prevention and Treatment Month

President, Secretary and Treasurer for next year of service needs to be reported to your club, district and RI as soon as possible. Follow their guidelines and procedures for sharing this information.

Encourage the President-Elect to register and attend PETS.

Include this information in your club bulletin this month, and discuss it one meeting:

The sixth Area of Focus for the Rotary Foundation Global Grants Program is Economic and Community Development. Below is a summary of how they see this best undertaken in developing countries:

Rotary supports activities and training that reduce the cause and effect of disease.

Areas of Focus Policy Statements

1. TRF enables Rotarians to prevent disease and promote health by:

2. Improving the capacity of local health care professionals;

3. Promoting disease prevention programs, with the goal of limiting the spread of communicable diseases and reducing the incidences of and complications from non-communicable diseases;

4. Enhancing the health infrastructure of local communities;

5. Educating and mobilizing communities to help prevent the spread of major diseases;

6. Preventing physical disability resulting from disease or injury;

7. Supporting studies for career-minded professionals related to disease prevention and treatment.

Some ideas for Disease Prevention and Treatment Month

- This is the perfect time to highlight Rotary's work to eradicate polio. Remember that newer members will not necessarily know the history of this program;
- Ask a local doctor to speak to you about attitudes to vaccination in our community and the ramifications of that;
- Ask a dentist to speak to you about dental health.

- Hold a board meeting

Notes:

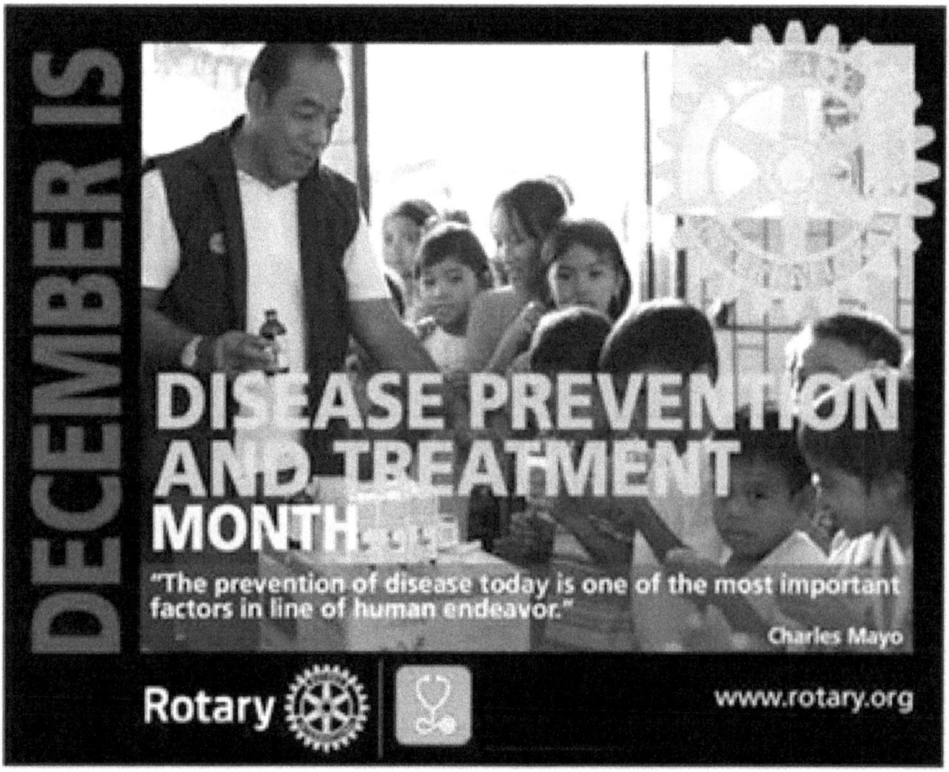
DECEMBER IS
DISEASE PREVENTION AND TREATMENT MONTH
"The prevention of disease today is one of the most important factors in line of human endeavor."
Charles Mayo
Rotary
www.rotary.org

Meeting Date _____

Program/Speaker _____

Invocation _____

Pledge _____

4 Way Test _____

Other Club Tradition _____

Other Club Tradition _____

Other Club Tradition _____

Other Club Tradition _____

Guests: _____

_____

_____

_____

Notes/Comments/Special Moments:

Meeting Date _____

Program/Speaker _____

Invocation _____

Pledge _____

4 Way Test _____

Other Club Tradition _____

Other Club Tradition _____

Other Club Tradition _____

Other Club Tradition _____

Guests: _____

_____

_____

_____

Notes/Comments/Special Moments:

Meeting Date _____

Program/Speaker _____

Invocation _____

Pledge _____

4 Way Test _____

Other Club Tradition _____

Other Club Tradition _____

Other Club Tradition _____

Other Club Tradition _____

Guests: _____

_____

_____

_____

Notes/Comments/Special Moments:

Meeting Date _____

Program/Speaker _____

Invocation _____

Pledge _____

4 Way Test _____

Other Club Tradition _____

Other Club Tradition _____

Other Club Tradition _____

Other Club Tradition _____

Guests: _____

_____

_____

_____

Notes/Comments/Special Moments:

Meeting Date _____

Program/Speaker _____

Invocation _____

Pledge _____

4 Way Test _____

Other Club Tradition _____

Other Club Tradition _____

Other Club Tradition _____

Other Club Tradition _____

Guests: _____

_____

_____

_____

Notes/Comments/Special Moments:

January - Vocational Service Month

By 31 January: Ensure Secretary / Treasurer has received Club Invoice and has arranged payment.	
***Register for the District Conference as soon as it opens. Continue to encourage attendance by as many members and partners as possible.	
Vocational Service focuses on: • Adhering to and promoting the highest ethical standards in all occupations • Recognizing the value of all useful occupations, not just those that are pursued by Rotarians • Contributing one's vocational talents to meeting the needs of the community	
Some ideas for Vocational Service month: • Sponsor a Four-Way Test essay or speech competition for young people. • Get actively involved in providing career information for local school students • Use classification talks by club members for at least three club meeting programs during the year? • Recognize the importance of high ethical standards and public values by giving an award to honour an individual who exemplifies such traits? • Routinely provide a copy of The Four- Way Test and the Declaration of Rotarians in Businesses and Professions to all new club members as they join the club • Post the Four-Way Test on a prominent billboard in your community. • Sponsor an essay contest in which participants describe how they can apply The Four Way Test to their lives. This could be for both youths and adults. • Introduce a "classification talk" series in which each member gives a five-minute talk on his or her vocation. These presentations give members the chance to learn the inner workings of jobs other than their own, including the various problems that arise and the solutions used to address them. • Help young people prepare for their careers by sponsoring a character building project, career day, job shadowing day, or mentorship program.	

Hold a board meeting	
Hold a Club Assembly	

Notes:

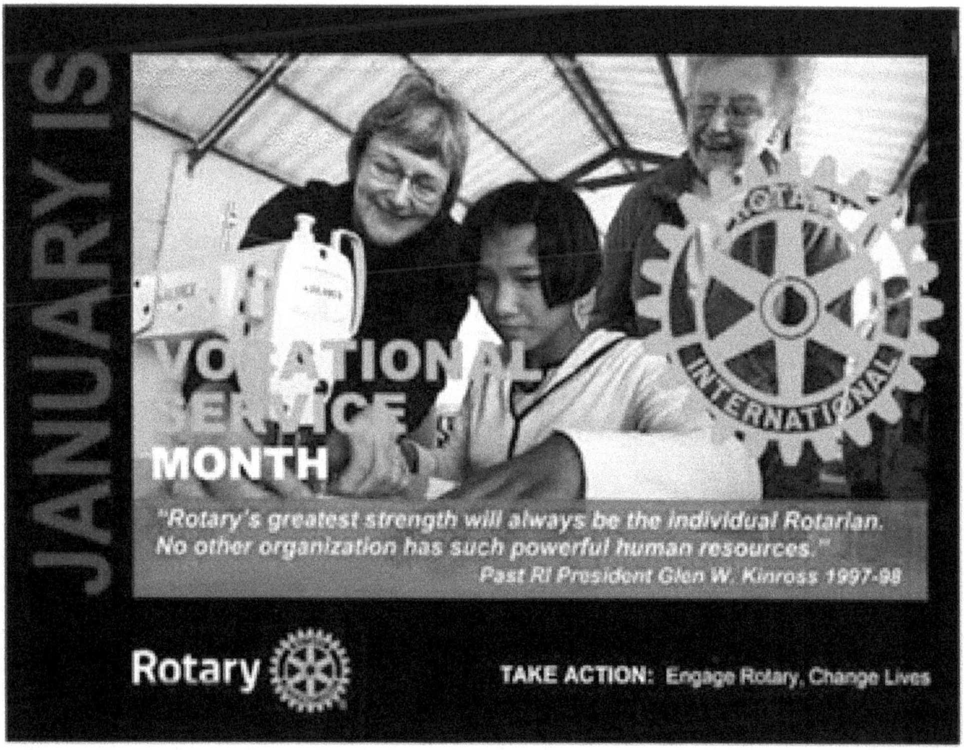

Meeting Date _____

Program/Speaker _____

Invocation _____

Pledge _____

4 Way Test _____

Other Club Tradition _____

Other Club Tradition _____

Other Club Tradition _____

Other Club Tradition _____

Guests: _____

_____

_____

_____

Notes/Comments/Special Moments:

Meeting Date _____

Program/Speaker _____

Invocation _____

Pledge _____

4 Way Test _____

Other Club Tradition _____

Other Club Tradition _____

Other Club Tradition _____

Other Club Tradition _____

Guests: _____

_____

_____

_____

Notes/Comments/Special Moments:

Meeting Date _____

Program/Speaker _____

Invocation _____

Pledge _____

4 Way Test _____

Other Club Tradition _____

Other Club Tradition _____

Other Club Tradition _____

Other Club Tradition _____

Guests: _____

_____

_____

_____

Notes/Comments/Special Moments:

Meeting Date _____

Program/Speaker _____

Invocation _____

Pledge _____

4 Way Test _____

Other Club Tradition _____

Other Club Tradition _____

Other Club Tradition _____

Other Club Tradition _____

Guests: _____

_____

_____

_____

Notes/Comments/Special Moments:

Meeting Date _____

Program/Speaker _____

Invocation _____

Pledge _____

4 Way Test _____

Other Club Tradition _____

Other Club Tradition _____

Other Club Tradition _____

Other Club Tradition _____

Guests: _____

_____

_____

_____

Notes/Comments/Special Moments:

February - Peace and Conflict Prevention/ Resolution Month

Include this information in your club bulletin this month, and discuss it one meeting:

The first Area of Focus for the Rotary Foundation Global Grants Program is Peace and Conflict prevention / Resolution. Below is a summary of how they see this best undertaken in developing countries:

Rotary supports the training, education, and practice of peace and conflict prevention and resolution.

Area of Focus Statement of Purpose and Goals

TRF enables Rotarians to promote the practice of peace and conflict prevention/ resolution by:

- Training leaders, including potential youth leaders, to prevent and mediate conflict;
- Supporting peace-building in communities and regions affected by conflict;
- Supporting studies for career-minded professionals related to peace and conflict prevention/resolution.

FEBRUARY IS

PEACE AND CONFLICT PREVENTION/RESOLUTION MONTH

"Imagine all the people living life in peace..."

John Lennon

Rotary

www.rotary.org

Ideas for Peace & Conflict Prevention / Resolution Month:

- During this month, Rotary clubs focus on projects and programs that promote peace and reduce conflict in our communities and around the world.
- Ask someone to address the club about the psychological effects of conflict;
- Have a speaker on reducing alcohol related conflict amongst young people; or ask a group of young people come to speak to you about the issue and how it could be addressed from their perspective;
- Educate youth on preventive measures to avoid conflict;
- Seek a sister club from another part of the world;
- Put some money towards a ShelterBox or some other Rotary partnered service project;
- Find out about, take part in training programs or campaigns to address negative social dynamics in a community, including but not limited to overcoming racial differences;
- Learn about Rotary's Peace and Conflict Resolution programs;
- Contribute to a district scholarship for graduate-level study in programs related to peace and conflict prevention/resolution.
- Have a quiz using a powerpoint to see how many members will recognise flags from around the world. The same thing can be done with photos of cities, or monuments, or famous people, anything that makes us think about other people in other places.
- Pause each meeting to remember Rotary's quest for goodwill, peace and understanding among people of the world.
- Update your club's goal achievements on Rotary Club Central.

Hold a board meeting

Notes:

Meeting Date _____

Program/Speaker _____

Invocation _____

Pledge _____

4 Way Test _____

Other Club Tradition _____

Other Club Tradition _____

Other Club Tradition _____

Other Club Tradition _____

Guests: _____

_____

_____

_____

Notes/Comments/Special Moments:

Meeting Date _____

Program/Speaker _____

Invocation _____

Pledge _____

4 Way Test _____

Other Club Tradition _____

Other Club Tradition _____

Other Club Tradition _____

Other Club Tradition _____

Guests: _____

_____

_____

_____

Notes/Comments/Special Moments:

Meeting Date _____

Program/Speaker _____

Invocation _____

Pledge _____

4 Way Test _____

Other Club Tradition _____

Other Club Tradition _____

Other Club Tradition _____

Other Club Tradition _____

Guests: _____

_____

_____

_____

Notes/Comments/Special Moments:

Meeting Date _____

Program/Speaker _____

Invocation _____

Pledge _____

4 Way Test _____

Other Club Tradition _____

Other Club Tradition _____

Other Club Tradition _____

Other Club Tradition _____

Guests: _____

_____

_____

_____

Notes/Comments/Special Moments:

Meeting Date _____

Program/Speaker _____

Invocation _____

Pledge _____

4 Way Test _____

Other Club Tradition _____

Other Club Tradition _____

Other Club Tradition _____

Other Club Tradition _____

Guests: _____

_____

_____

_____

Notes/Comments/Special Moments:

March- Water & Sanitation Month	
**Make final arrangements to attend the District Conference.	
Include this information in your club bulletin this month, and discuss it one meeting:	
The third Area of Focus for the Rotary Foundation Global Grants Program is Water and Sanitation. Below is a summary of how they see this best undertaken in developing countries:	
Rotary supports activities and training to provide access to safe drinking water and basic sanitation.	
Area of Focus Statement of Purpose and Goals	
TRF enables Rotarians to ensure that people have sustainable access to water and sanitation by:	
1. Providing equitable community access to safe water, improved sanitation and hygiene;	
2. Strengthening the ability of communities to develop, fund and maintain sustainable water and sanitation systems;	
3. Supporting programs that enhance communities' awareness of the benefits of safe water, sanitation and hygiene;	
4. Supporting studies for career-minded professionals related to water and sanitation	
Ideas for Water and Sanitation Month: • See if someone can come to speak to you about their water project. • Find examples of projects in this field in your District and highlight them one meeting. • Explore the water situation in your local community - do you have plenty, what is its future, what risks are there to deal with in the future?	
Hold a board meeting	

Notes:

MARCH IS
WATER AND SANITATION
MONTH
"Clean water, the essence of life and a birthright for everyone, must become available to all people now."
Rotary
www.rotary.org

Meeting Date _____

Program/Speaker _____

Invocation _____

Pledge _____

4 Way Test _____

Other Club Tradition _____

Other Club Tradition _____

Other Club Tradition _____

Other Club Tradition _____

Guests: _____

_____

_____

_____

Notes/Comments/Special Moments:

Meeting Date _____

Program/Speaker _____

Invocation _____

Pledge _____

4 Way Test _____

Other Club Tradition _____

Other Club Tradition _____

Other Club Tradition _____

Other Club Tradition _____

Guests: _____

_____

_____

_____

Notes/Comments/Special Moments:

Meeting Date _____

Program/Speaker _____

Invocation _____

Pledge _____

4 Way Test _____

Other Club Tradition _____

Other Club Tradition _____

Other Club Tradition _____

Other Club Tradition _____

Guests: _____

_____

_____

_____

Notes/Comments/Special Moments:

Meeting Date _____

Program/Speaker _____

Invocation _____

Pledge _____

4 Way Test _____

Other Club Tradition _____

Other Club Tradition _____

Other Club Tradition _____

Other Club Tradition _____

Guests: _____

_____

_____

_____

Notes/Comments/Special Moments:

Meeting Date _____

Program/Speaker _____

Invocation _____

Pledge _____

4 Way Test _____

Other Club Tradition _____

Other Club Tradition _____

Other Club Tradition _____

Other Club Tradition _____

Guests: _____

_____

_____

_____

Notes/Comments/Special Moments:

April - Maternal and Child Health Month	
**Attend the District Conference this month or next.	
Include this information in your club bulletin this month, and discuss it one meeting: The fourth Area of Focus for the Rotary Foundation Global Grants Program is Maternal and Child Health. Below is a summary of how they see this best undertaken in developing countries: Rotary supports activities and training to improve maternal health and reduce child mortality for children under five. **Area of Focus Statement of Purpose and Goals** TRF enables Rotarians to improve the health of mothers and their children by 1. Reducing the mortality and morbidity rate for children under the age of five; 2. Reducing the maternal mortality and morbidity rate; 3. Improving access to essential medical services, trained community health leaders and health care providers for mothers and their children; 4. Supporting studies for career-minded professionals related to maternal and child health.	
Ideas for Maternal and Child Health month: • Ask members to locate an article from the current or past Rotarian that highlights the work of Rotary in the field of Maternal and Child health; • Write about this topic in your local newspaper; • Find out about the Days for Girls project (www.daysforgirls.org) and consider putting together some items for this wonderful program; • Have a local doctor speak to you about any issues.	
Plan the club Changeover/Installation. See that the Annual Report will be completed on time, and that any annual awards are organized.	
Check with your treasurer that the books will be ready for audit as soon as possible after the end of June.	
Hold a board meeting	
Hold a Club Assembly	

Notes

Meeting Date _____

Program/Speaker _____

Invocation _____

Pledge _____

4 Way Test _____

Other Club Tradition _____

Other Club Tradition _____

Other Club Tradition _____

Other Club Tradition _____

Guests: _____

_____

_____

_____

Notes/Comments/Special Moments:

Meeting Date _____

Program/Speaker _____

Invocation _____

Pledge _____

4 Way Test _____

Other Club Tradition _____

Other Club Tradition _____

Other Club Tradition _____

Other Club Tradition _____

Guests: _____

_____

_____

_____

Notes/Comments/Special Moments:

Meeting Date _____

Program/Speaker _____

Invocation _____

Pledge _____

4 Way Test _____

Other Club Tradition _____

Other Club Tradition _____

Other Club Tradition _____

Other Club Tradition _____

Guests: _____

_____

_____

_____

Notes/Comments/Special Moments:

Meeting Date _____

Program/Speaker _____

Invocation _____

Pledge _____

4 Way Test _____

Other Club Tradition _____

Other Club Tradition _____

Other Club Tradition _____

Other Club Tradition _____

Guests: _____

_____

_____

_____

Notes/Comments/Special Moments:

Meeting Date _____

Program/Speaker _____

Invocation _____

Pledge _____

4 Way Test _____

Other Club Tradition _____

Other Club Tradition _____

Other Club Tradition _____

Other Club Tradition _____

Guests: _____

_____

_____

_____

Notes/Comments/Special Moments:

May - Youth Service Month	
Ideas for Youth Services month: • Recognize students who exemplify Rotary's ideals of service by offering awards and scholarships for exemplary young people in your community • Involve local youth in fundraising efforts that support projects for young people in the community or around the world • Support youth through community service projects such as donating books and dictionaries to school libraries • If you have a teacher Rotarian, consider starting an Interact club in the teacher's school. • Use your meetings to make sure all members know a little at least about all the youth programs - YEP, RYLA, Interact • Ask a current or former YEP student to speak to the club about their experiences and how they have impacted their life	
Confirm with the incoming President about the Changeover/ Installation function - what will be your role, their role, what will you both have to do	
See that invitations to the club Changeover/Installation are sent out	
Make decisions with your club members about the disbursement of funds at the end of your year.	
Hold a board meeting	

Notes:

MAY IS
YOUTH
SERVICE
MONTH
"We cannot talk about the future without talking about children. They are our future." - PRIP James L. Lacy 1998-99
Rotary
YOUTH
www.rotary.org

Meeting Date _____

Program/Speaker _____

Invocation _____

Pledge _____

4 Way Test _____

Other Club Tradition _____

Other Club Tradition _____

Other Club Tradition _____

Other Club Tradition _____

Guests: _____

_____

_____

_____

Notes/Comments/Special Moments:

Meeting Date _____

Program/Speaker _____

Invocation _____

Pledge _____

4 Way Test _____

Other Club Tradition _____

Other Club Tradition _____

Other Club Tradition _____

Other Club Tradition _____

Guests: _____

_____

_____

_____

Notes/Comments/Special Moments:

Meeting Date _____

Program/Speaker _____

Invocation _____

Pledge _____

4 Way Test _____

Other Club Tradition _____

Other Club Tradition _____

Other Club Tradition _____

Other Club Tradition _____

Guests: _____

_____

_____

_____

Notes/Comments/Special Moments:

Meeting Date _____

Program/Speaker _____

Invocation _____

Pledge _____

4 Way Test _____

Other Club Tradition _____

Other Club Tradition _____

Other Club Tradition _____

Other Club Tradition _____

Guests: _____

_____

_____

_____

Notes/Comments/Special Moments:

Meeting Date _____

Program/Speaker _____

Invocation _____

Pledge _____

4 Way Test _____

Other Club Tradition _____

Other Club Tradition _____

Other Club Tradition _____

Other Club Tradition _____

Guests: _____

_____

_____

_____

Notes/Comments/Special Moments:

June - Rotary Fellowships Month	
Have everything ready to hand over to the incoming board.	
Hold a combined board meeting to discuss the hand-over.	
The Club Changeover/Installation!!! Almost there!!!	
Ideas for Rotary Fellowship Month: • Learn more about Rotary Fellowships. How to get involved? Rotary Fellowships are autonomous, international groups of Rotarians, Rotarian spouses, and Rotaractors who join together to enjoy fellowship through a shared interest, make new friends around the world, explore new opportunities for service, have fun and enhance their Rotary experience • Consult the Rotary Fellowship Directory (Google it) to get in touch with group(s) you are interested in • Consider joining a Rotary Fellowship that addresses your interest. • Have a member of a Fellowship speak about how this contributes to their Rotary experience	
Update your club's goal achievements on Rotary Club Central.	

Notes:

JUNE DESIGNATION IS

ROTARY
FELLOWSHIPS
MONTH

"The foundation upon which Rotary is built is friendship; on no less firm foundation could it have stood."

Paul P Harris, 1935

Rotary

TAKE ACTION: rotaryfellowships@rotary.org

Meeting Date _____

Program/Speaker _____

Invocation _____

Pledge _____

4 Way Test _____

Other Club Tradition _____

Other Club Tradition _____

Other Club Tradition _____

Other Club Tradition _____

Guests: _____

_____

_____

_____

Notes/Comments/Special Moments:

Meeting Date _____

Program/Speaker _____

Invocation _____

Pledge _____

4 Way Test _____

Other Club Tradition _____

Other Club Tradition _____

Other Club Tradition _____

Other Club Tradition _____

Guests: _____

_____

_____

_____

Notes/Comments/Special Moments:

Meeting Date _____

Program/Speaker _____

Invocation _____

Pledge _____

4 Way Test _____

Other Club Tradition _____

Other Club Tradition _____

Other Club Tradition _____

Other Club Tradition _____

Guests: _____

_____

_____

_____

Notes/Comments/Special Moments:

Meeting Date _____

Program/Speaker _____

Invocation _____

Pledge _____

4 Way Test _____

Other Club Tradition _____

Other Club Tradition _____

Other Club Tradition _____

Other Club Tradition _____

Guests: _____

_____

_____

_____

Notes/Comments/Special Moments:

Meeting Date _____

Program/Speaker _____

Invocation _____

Pledge _____

4 Way Test _____

Other Club Tradition _____

Other Club Tradition _____

Other Club Tradition _____

Other Club Tradition _____

Guests: _____

_____

_____

_____

Notes/Comments/Special Moments:

"The single biggest way to impact an organization is to focus on leadership development. There is almost no limit to the potential of an organization that recruits good people, raises them up as leaders and continually develops them."

-John Maxwell

In Conclusion

Now that you are the Immediate Past President doesn't mean your job is done.

Immediate Past President

The Immediate Past President's role is to use his/her knowledge and experience on the Board to assist the current President. He/she also performs several important functions for the Board.

1. Provides advice and leadership to the Board of Directors regarding past practices and other matters to assist the Board in governing the Club.

2. Supports the president and the President-Elect on an as-needed basis.

3. Performs the duties of the President in the absence or disability of the President.

4. Mentors the president and board and provide transitional support to the board and club.

It's important to the ongoing success of your club to develop your club's leadership pipeline. Establishing a leadership pipeline ensures that the club's vision, plan, organizational structure, relationships and most importantly knowledge are carried on with minimal disruption.

Key Concepts of Succession Planning

- **Apply the apprentice leadership method** This style of leadership involves teaching a new leader the role through supported practice. The predecessor gives the successor the expectations of the position, the tools for success and mentoring in the early days of the transition.
- **Identify leaders or "doers" in your club** Be constantly looking for the right people in your club to assume leadership positions in the future. Begin engaging them in club activities and offer them opportunities to develop their leadership skills.
- **Recognize your leaders** This recognition should be timely, appropriate and immediate in order to be effective. This will encourage other members to consider assuming leadership positions.

www.ingramcontent.com/pod-product-compliance
Lightning Source LLC
Chambersburg PA
CBHW051842090426
42736CB00011B/1923